BRUSSELS TRAVEL GUIDE 2023

The Most Updated Travel Guide for Navigating Brussels' Must-See Gems and Local Hotspots

GW00503257

PAMELA JADEN

Table of Contents

Accommodations, Places of interest and Airport.

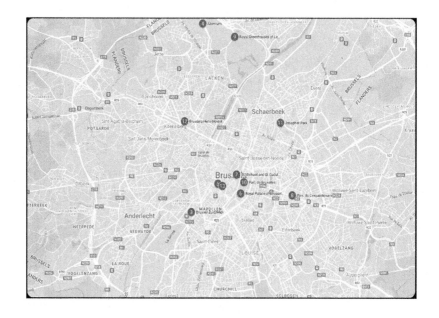

Introduction to Brussels

Travel is fun and recess, we need it. In a realm where history merges with modernity, where cobblestone streets whisper tales of bygone eras, there exists a city that defies expectations and captivates the soul. Welcome to Brussels, a place where the ordinary becomes extraordinary, and every step unravels a new layer of wonder.

Imagine yourself standing amidst the awe-inspiring Grand-Place, its ornate architecture reaching towards the heavens, immersing you in a symphony of beauty and splendor. As you wander through its enchanting neighborhoods, you'll discover a kaleidoscope of cultures, where the old and the new coexist in perfect harmony.

Brussels is a city that ignites the senses, where aromas of freshly baked waffles fill the air and the taste of velvety chocolates dances upon your palate.

It is a haven for art enthusiasts, with its world-class museums and galleries that breathe life into the canvas of human imagination.

But Brussels is more than just a city; it is a state of mind. It is a place where dreams take flight, where inspiration is found at every turn. Let this travel guidebook be your gateway to the mind-blowing experiences that await you, as you unlock the secrets of Brussels and create memories that will leave you forever transformed. Get ready to embark on a journey of the heart and soul, where the unimaginable becomes a reality, and Brussels unveils its true magic.

About Brussels

Brussels, the capital city of Belgium, is a captivating destination that offers a perfect blend of history, culture, and modernity. Situated in the heart of Europe, this cosmopolitan metropolis is known for its stunning architecture, vibrant art scene, delicious cuisine, and warm hospitality.

The city's rich history dates back centuries, evident in its magnificent landmarks and UNESCO-listed historic center. The iconic Grand-Place stands as a testament to Brussels' grandeur, with its ornate guildhalls and impressive City Hall. The Atomium, a futuristic structure originally built for the 1958 World Expo, symbolizes the city's innovative spirit. Brussels is a cultural hub, boasting a plethora of museums, art galleries, and theaters. Art enthusiasts will find themselves immersed in masterpieces at the Royal Museums of Fine Arts of Belgium, while comic book lovers can explore the Belgian Comic Strip Center. The city's diverse neighborhoods, such as the European Quarter and Marolles, offer a vibrant mix of cultures and experiences.

Indulging in Belgian cuisine is a must-do in Brussels. From indulgent chocolates and delicate waffles to savory moules-frites (mussels and fries) and the famous Belgian beers, the city's culinary scene is a delight for food lovers.

Brussels also serves as the political capital of the European Union, making it an important center for international diplomacy and governance. The European Parliament and other EU institutions are located here, contributing to the city's global significance.

Beyond the city limits, Brussels provides easy access to picturesque towns like Ghent, Bruges, and Antwerp, offering additional opportunities to explore the rich heritage and charm of Belgium.

Transportation in Brussels is efficient, with a well-connected public transportation system that includes trains, trams, and buses. Biking is also popular, with the city offering extensive cycling infrastructure.

Whether you're strolling through the cobblestone streets of the historic center, admiring the stunning architecture, or savoring the flavors of Belgian cuisine, Brussels offers a captivating experience that will leave a lasting impression. Its unique blend of tradition and modernity, coupled with a welcoming atmosphere, ensures that visitors are enchanted by all that this remarkable city has to offer.

A Brief History of Brussels and Brussels Today

Brussels has a rich and fascinating history that spans over a thousand years. It began as a small fortress town in the 10th century and gradually grew in importance, becoming a center of commerce and culture.

In the 15th century, Brussels became the capital of the Duchy of Brabant and experienced a period of prosperity and growth. The iconic Town Hall in the Grand-Place was constructed during this time, showcasing the city's architectural splendor.

Over the centuries, Brussels faced numerous challenges and changes. It was occupied by foreign powers, including the Spanish, French, and Dutch, and witnessed political turmoil and social unrest. In the 19th century, Belgium gained independence, and Brussels was established as the capital of the newly formed country.

In the 20th century, Brussels solidified its position as an important European city. It became the headquarters of several international organizations, including the European Union and NATO, further enhancing its global significance. The city underwent urban development, with the construction of modern buildings and the expansion of transportation infrastructure.

Brussels Today:

Today, Brussels is a vibrant and multicultural city that seamlessly blends tradition with modernity. It is known for its diverse population, with inhabitants from all corners of the globe contributing to its cosmopolitan atmosphere.

The city's historic center, with its stunning architecture and cobblestone streets, remains a major attraction. The Grand-Place, a UNESCO World Heritage site, is a focal point of Brussels' cultural and social life. Visitors can explore the maze-like streets of the Marolles district, indulge in the culinary delights of the Sainte-Catherine neighborhood, or immerse themselves in the European Quarter, home to the European Parliament and other EU institutions.

Brussels boasts an impressive array of cultural institutions, including world-class museums, art galleries, and theaters. The city's cultural calendar is filled with festivals, exhibitions, and performances, ensuring a vibrant and diverse cultural experience.

The culinary scene in Brussels is a highlight for food enthusiasts. From Michelin-starred restaurants to cozy brasseries and bustling food markets, the city offers a mouthwatering range of Belgian delicacies, including chocolates, waffles, and the famous Belgian beers.

Brussels continues to be a hub of political and diplomatic activity, hosting international conferences and events. Its strategic location in the heart of Europe makes it a convenient base for exploring other Belgian cities and neighboring countries.

With its blend of historical charm, modern dynamism, and international allure, Brussels has firmly established itself as a must-visit destination. Whether you're drawn to its captivating history, cultural treasures, gastronomic delights, or global significance, Brussels offers a unique and memorable experience that will leave a lasting impression.

Geography and Climate of Brussels

Geographically, Brussels is located in the central part of Belgium, serving as the capital city and the administrative center of the Brussels-Capital Region. Situated in the heart of Europe, it is well-connected to other major cities and countries, making it an ideal base for exploring the wider region.

Brussels lies within the larger geographical regions of Flanders and Wallonia, straddling the cultural and linguistic divide between Dutch-speaking Flanders to the north and French-speaking Wallonia to the south. This linguistic diversity adds to the city's unique character and cultural richness.

The city is situated on relatively flat terrain, with an average elevation of around 50 meters (164 feet) above sea level. The landscape is characterized by urban development, parks, and green spaces, providing a pleasant environment for residents and visitors alike.

As for the climate, Brussels experiences a temperate maritime climate, influenced by its proximity to the North Sea. Summers in Brussels are generally mild, with average high temperatures ranging from 20°C to 23°C (68°F to 73°F). Winters are cool, with average highs around 5°C (41°F). Rainfall is distributed fairly evenly throughout the year, and snowfall is not uncommon in winter, adding a touch of charm to the cityscape.

Being prepared for the weather is essential when visiting Brussels. Pack clothing suitable for various conditions, including layers for variable temperatures and precipitation. Comfortable walking shoes are recommended to explore the city's neighborhoods and attractions, as well as its extensive public transportation system.

With a favorable climate and diverse geography, Brussels offers a captivating backdrop for your explorations. From strolling through picturesque parks in spring and summer to witnessing the colorful autumn foliage or enjoying the cozy ambiance of winter, each season brings its own unique charm to the city.

Understanding the geography and climate of Brussels will help you plan your activities and make the most of your time in the city, ensuring a comfortable and enjoyable visit throughout the year.

Exploring Brussels Neighborhoods

From the iconic Grand-Place to the charming streets of Marolles, each neighborhood has its own unique character and attractions, promising unforgettable experiences for every traveler.

1. **Grand-Place and the Historic Center:** Step into the heart of Brussels as you explore the UNESCO-listed Grand-Place. Marvel at the Gothic and Baroque architecture, visit the impressive Town Hall, and soak up the historic atmosphere of this iconic square. Wander through the cobblestone streets, discovering charming shops, delightful cafés, and historical landmarks.

2. **European Quarter:** Immerse yourself in the political hub of Europe in the European Quarter. Visit the European Parliament, Commission, and Council buildings, and gain insight into the workings of the European

Union. Explore the green spaces of Parc Léopold and enjoy the modern architecture that defines this cosmopolitan neighborhood.

3. **Sablon and Marolles:** Indulge your senses in the elegant district of Sablon, known for its upscale boutiques, antique shops, and renowned chocolatiers. Discover the treasures of the daily flea market at Place du Jeu de Balle in Marolles, and experience the bohemian ambiance of this artistic neighborhood.

4. **Saint-Gilles and Ixelles:** Experience the vibrant and eclectic energy of Saint-Gilles and Ixelles. Stroll through the bustling neighborhoods, filled with trendy boutiques, art galleries, and delightful cafés. Explore the picturesque ponds of Ixelles and immerse yourself in the lively atmosphere of Avenue Louise and Place du Chatelain.

5. **Uccle and Forest:** Escape to the tranquil districts of Uccle and Forest, where you can enjoy the serenity of expansive parks and lush greenery. Explore the beautiful Wolvendael Park, unwind in the peaceful surroundings of Duden Park, and discover the hidden gems tucked away in these peaceful residential neighborhoods.

6. **Schaerbeek and Josaphat:** Discover the cultural diversity and architectural splendor of Schaerbeek. Marvel at the Art Nouveau buildings, explore the vibrant Josaphat Park, and immerse yourself in the vibrant markets and local atmosphere of this multicultural district.

7. **Anderlecht and Molenbeek:** Uncover the lesser-known neighborhoods of Anderlecht and Molenbeek, where tradition meets modernity. Explore the bustling Anderlecht

Market, soak up the local vibe, and experience the multicultural communities that thrive in these dynamic districts.

Beyond Brussels: Expand your horizons and venture beyond the city limits to explore the wonders that lie in the surrounding region. Take day trips to charming towns like Ghent, Bruges, and Antwerp, where medieval architecture and cultural heritage await. Delve into the rich history of Waterloo or embrace the natural beauty of the Belgian countryside.

This comprehensive guide will accompany you on your journey, offering insights into each neighborhood's highlights, local recommendations, and cultural treasures. Whether you're a history buff, art enthusiast, food lover, or simply a curious traveler, Brussels and its captivating neighborhoods have something for everyone. Get ready to embark on an unforgettable adventure creating memories that will last a lifetime through the diverse neighborhoods of Brussels and the enchanting destinations that await beyond its borders.

Chapter 1: Planning Your Trip to Brussels

Brussels offers a wealth of attractions, so it's important to plan your itinerary based on the length of your trip.When it comes to planning your trip to Brussels, there are various factors to put in mind to ensure a smooth and breath-taking experience. Here are some essential tips to help you make the most of your visit:

- **Research and Plan:**

Gather information about Brussels, its attractions, and points of interest.

Determine the number of days you would stay and create a rough itinerary.

Consider your interests and prioritize the places you wish to visit.

- **Travel Documents and Insurance:**

Check passport validity and visa requirements for your country.

Try to get travel insurance to protect against unforeseen events.

- **Flights and Transportation:**

Look for the best flight deals and book your tickets ahead.

Consider the options for transportation within Brussels, such as trains, trams, and buses.Research transportation passes or cards for convenient travel.

- **Accommodation:**

Decide on the type of accommodation that suits your needs and budget for your travel.

Research different neighborhoods and choose the one that aligns with your preferences.

Book your accommodation well in advance to secure the best options.

- **Local Customs and Etiquette:**

Familiarize yourself with the local customs and etiquette in Brussels.

Learn a few basic phrases in French and Dutch to communicate with locals.

- **Money Matters:**

Exchange currency or withdraw cash from ATMs upon arrival.

Inform your bank about your travel plans to avoid any issues with the use of your card.

Keep track of your expenses and set a budget for your trip.

Ten (10) things to know before visiting Brussels

Here are ten (10) things to know before visiting Brussels:

1. **Brussels is the capital of Belgium.** It's a small city, but it's packed with history, culture, and delicious food.

2. **The Brussels' official languages are French and Dutch.** However, English is widely spoken, so you shouldn't have any trouble getting around.

3. **The weather in Brussels can be unpredictable.** It can be sunny one day and rainy the next, so it's important to pack for all types of weather.

4. **Brussels is a foodie city.** There are many delicious restaurants to choose from, serving everything from Belgian waffles to fine dining.

5. **Brussels is a beer city.** Belgium is known for its beer, and there are many breweries and bars to visit in Brussels.

6. **Brussels is a chocolate city.** Belgium is also known for its chocolate, and there are many chocolate shops to visit in Brussels.

7. **Brussels is a historic city.** There are many historical sites to visit in Brussels, including the Grand Place, the Manneken Pis, and the Atomium.

8. **Brussels is a cultural city.** There are many museums, art galleries, and theaters to visit in Brussels.

9. **Brussels is a convenient city.** There are many public transportation options available, making it easy to get around the city.

10. **Brussels is a safe city.** Brussels is a relatively safe city, but it's always a good idea to be aware of your surroundings.

Here are some additional tips for first-time visitors to Brussels:

- **Book your accommodations in advance.** Brussels is a popular tourist destination, so it's a good idea to book your accommodations in advance, especially if you're traveling during peak season.

- **Get a Brussels Card.** The Brussels Card gives you free admission to many of the city's attractions, as well as discounts on public transportation and other activities.
- **Use the hop-on, hop-off bus.** The hop-on, hop-off bus is a great way to see the city and get to your desired attractions quickly and easily.
- **Take a walk through the Grand Place.** The Grand Place is one of the most beautiful squares in the world, and it's a must-see for any visitor to Brussels.
- **Visit the Manneken Pis.** The Manneken Pis is one of the most famous statues in the world, and it's a must-see for any visitor to Brussels.

- **Go to the Atomium.** The Atomium is a giant steel structure that represents an iron crystal magnified 165 billion times. It's a must-see for any visitor to Brussels.
- **Try some Belgian waffles.** Belgian waffles are a delicious and popular snack in Belgium. They're made with a special batter and cooked in a special iron.
- **Have a beer at a local brewery.** Belgium is known for its beer, so you should definitely try some at a local brewery.
- **Enjoy the nightlife in Brussels.** Brussels has a vibrant nightlife scene, so you're sure to find something to your liking.

Five (5) things to avoid.

Here are five (5) things to avoid before you travel to Brussels:

1. **Avoid traveling during peak season.** Brussels is a popular tourist destination, so it can be crowded and expensive during peak season (June-August). If you can, try to travel during the shoulder seasons (April-May, September-October) or the off-season (November-March).

2. **Avoid getting scammed.** There are a few scams that are common in Brussels, such as the "broken phone" scam and the "fake taxi" scam. Be aware of these scams and be careful when you're out and about.

3. **Avoid eating at tourist traps.** There are a lot of tourist traps in Brussels that serve overpriced and mediocre food. Do some research before you go and find some good restaurants that are off the beaten path.

4. **Avoid drinking too much beer.** Belgium is known for its beer, and it's easy to get carried

away. If you're not used to drinking beer, be careful not to drink too much.

5. **Avoid getting lost.** Brussels can be a confusing city, especially if you're not familiar with it. If you do get lost, don't panic. Just ask someone for directions or use a map app.

Here are some additional tips:

- **Be aware of your surroundings.** This is a good rule of thumb for any city, but it's especially important in Brussels. There have been a few terrorist attacks in Brussels in recent years, so it's important to be aware of your surroundings and take precautions.

- **Keep your valuables safe.** Don't carry your passport, money, or other valuables with you when you're out and about. Leave them in your hotel safe or in a locked bag.

- **Use common sense.** Don't go to sketchy areas alone, and don't accept drinks from strangers. If you feel unsafe, trust your instincts and get out of the situation.

When to Visit Brussels

- **Weather and Seasons:**

Understand the climate of Brussels throughout the year.

Summers (June to August) are generally warm, while **winters** (December to February) are cold and can be rainy.

Spring (March to May) and **autumn** (September to November) offer mild temperatures and less crowds.

- **Festivals and Events:**

Brussels hosts a variety of festivals and events throughout the year.

Consider the festivals and events happening in Brussels during your preferred travel dates.

Consider timing your visit to coincide with events like the Brussels Jazz Marathon in May, Belgian Beer Weekend in September.

The Ommegang Pageant in July and the Winter Wonders Christmas Market in December are popular attractions.

- **Peak and Off-Peak Seasons**:

Brussels experiences high tourist traffic during summer and around major holidays.

Consider visiting during shoulder seasons (spring and autumn) for pleasant weather and fewer crowds.

Budget Considerations:

Off-peak seasons often offer better deals on flights and accommodations.

Research discounts or special offers available during specific times of the year.

- **Personal Preferences:**

Determine your preferred travel atmosphere. Some travelers enjoy the buzz of summer crowds, while others prefer a quieter experience.

Consider your interests, such as art, history, or outdoor activities, and choose a time when related attractions are available.

By planning your trip to Brussels thoroughly and choosing the best time to visit, you can optimize your experience and make the most of your time in this captivating city. Whether you prefer vibrant festivals, pleasant weather, or a more budget-friendly trip, Brussels has something to offer throughout the year.

Packing Checklist

Clothing

- **Layers:** Brussels can have a wide range of temperatures, so it's important to pack layers so you can adjust to the weather. A **warm coat**, **scarf**, and **gloves** are essential for the winter months. For the summer, **pack light, breathable clothing** like **shorts, t-shirts**, and **skirts**.

- **Dress shoes:** You'll want to pack a pair of dress shoes for going out to dinner or other special occasions.
- **Comfortable shoes:** You'll also want to pack a pair of comfortable shoes for walking around the city. Sneakers or walking shoes are an excellent choice.

Accessories

- **Hat:** A hat is essential for keeping your head warm in the winter.
- **Sunglasses:** Sunglasses are a must-have for sunny days in Brussels, a reusable water bottle and a day bag for exploring,

- **Rain gear:** Brussels can get rainy, so it's a good idea to pack a raincoat or umbrella.
- **Travel pillow:** A travel pillow can help sleep on long flights or train rides.
- **Laptop:** If you're planning on doing any work while you're in Brussels, be sure to pack your laptop.
- **Camera:** Brussels is a beautiful city, so you'll want to pack a camera to capture all your memories.
- **Luggage lock:** A luggage lock can help keep your belongings safe while you're traveling.

Chapter 2: Getting to And Around Brussels

Getting to Brussels by Air

Brussels, being a major European capital, is well-served by international airlines and has excellent connectivity. If you're planning to visit Brussels and wondering how to reach the city by air, this guide will provide you with essential information and tips to make your journey smooth and hassle-free with excellent international connectivity and multiple airport options, reaching Brussels by air has never been easier.

Brussels Airport (BRU):

- Brussels Airport, also known as Zaventem Airport, is the primary international airport serving Brussels.

- Located approximately 12 kilometers (7.5 miles) northeast of the city center, it is well-connected to major cities around the world.

- Many major airlines operate flights to Brussels Airport, offering a wide range of options for travelers.

Charleroi Airport (CRL):

- Brussels South Charleroi Airport, commonly referred to as Charleroi Airport, is another airport serving Brussels, located about 46 kilometers (29 miles) south of the city center.

- Charleroi Airport mainly serves low-cost carriers and is a hub for budget airlines like Ryanair.

- It offers a cost-effective option for travelers looking for cheaper flights to Brussels.

International Connectivity:

- Brussels Airport has direct flights from numerous major cities across Europe, North America, Africa, the Middle East, and Asia.

- Airlines such as Brussels Airlines, Lufthansa, British Airways, Air France, and many others operate regular scheduled flights to Brussels.

- Charleroi Airport offers flights from various European cities, including popular destinations like Barcelona, Rome, Budapest, and more.

Ground Transportation from the Airports:

- From Brussels Airport, there are several transportation options to reach the city center. The fastest and most convenient option is the direct train service, which takes approximately 20 minutes.

- Charleroi Airport offers shuttle buses that connect the airport to Brussels Midi/Zuid train station, from where you can easily reach the city center.

Traveling to Brussels by air offers convenience and efficiency, allowing you to reach the city quickly and comfortably. Whether you choose the main Brussels Airport or opt for the budget-friendly Charleroi Airport, both provide excellent options for international travelers. Prepare for an exciting journey as you embark on your adventure to explore the vibrant and historic city of Brussels.

Traveling to Brussels by Train

A Convenient and Scenic Journey

If you're considering a trip to Brussels, traveling by train is an excellent option that offers convenience, comfort, and the opportunity to enjoy scenic views along the way. With its central location in Europe and well-connected rail network, Brussels is easily accessible from neighboring countries and major

European cities. In this section of the Brussels Travel Guide 2023, we will provide you with essential information and tips for a seamless train journey to the captivating capital of Belgium.

Traveling to Brussels by train offers several advantages. It allows you to avoid the hassle of airport security checks and long boarding times, while providing a comfortable and relaxing journey. Here's what you need to know:

- **International Train Connections:** Brussels benefits from its central location in Europe, with excellent train connections from neighboring countries and major European cities. High-speed trains, such as the Eurostar, Thalys, and TGV, operate regular services to Brussels from cities like London, Paris, Amsterdam, and Cologne. These trains offer convenient and direct routes, allowing you to reach Brussels easily and efficiently.

- **Brussels-Midi/Zuid Station:** Brussels' main train station, Brussels-Midi/Zuid, is a major hub for international and domestic train services. Located in the heart of the city, it offers convenient connections to other parts of Brussels and beyond. Upon arrival at Brussels-Midi/Zuid Station, you'll find various facilities and services, including ticket counters, information desks, luggage storage, and shops.

- **Train Ticket Options:** To make your train journey to Brussels smooth and cost-effective, it's advisable to purchase your tickets in advance. This allows you to secure the best fares and availability. You can explore different ticket options, including standard fares, discounted fares, and rail passes for multi-city or multi-country travel. Online ticketing platforms and official railway websites are convenient places to purchase tickets.

- **Comfort and Amenities:** Trains to Brussels are known for their comfort, offering spacious seating, ample legroom, and onboard amenities. Depending on the train service, you may find features such as Wi-Fi connectivity, power outlets, and even dining cars where you can enjoy a meal or snack during your journey. Sit back, relax, and enjoy the comfort of train travel as you make your way to Brussels.

- **Border Crossings:** If traveling from another European country to Brussels, be prepared for border crossings. While most train journeys within the European Union are seamless, some may involve passport checks and immigration procedures. Make sure to keep your passport and travel documents easily accessible to ensure a smooth transition at the borders.

- **Scenic Routes:** One of the highlights of traveling to Brussels by train is the opportunity to enjoy scenic views of the countryside along the way. As the train passes through picturesque landscapes, rolling hills, and charming towns, take advantage of the large windows to immerse yourself in the beauty of the journey. Capture memorable photos and relish the enchanting sights en route to Brussels.

- **Planning Tips:** To make your train journey to Brussels as smooth as possible, it's important to plan ahead. Check train schedules and plan your journey in advance to ensure timely connections. Arrive at the train station early to allow sufficient time for ticket validation and boarding. Familiarize yourself with the layout of Brussels-Midi/Zuid Station to navigate easily upon arrival and find your way to your accommodation or desired attractions.

Connecting to the City Center: Brussels-Midi/Zuid Station is conveniently located, providing easy access to the city center. Upon arrival, you can utilize the public transportation options available, such as the metro, trams, or buses, to reach your accommodation or desired attractions. Brussels has an efficient and well-connected public transportation system that allows you to explore the city and its surroundings with ease.

- **Day Trips from Brussels by Train:** Brussels serves as an excellent base for day trips to nearby cities and attractions. With its central location and extensive train network, you can easily explore destinations like Bruges, Ghent, Antwerp, and more. Consider taking short train rides to discover the rich cultural heritage, architectural wonders, and historical charm of these neighboring cities.

Traveling to Brussels by train offers a convenient, comfortable, and scenic journey that allows you to make the most of your travel experience. Whether you're arriving from a nearby European city or embarking on an intercontinental train adventure, the railways provide an efficient and enjoyable way to reach Brussels. Follow the tips in this guide to plan your train journey to Brussels, and get ready to explore the captivating capital of Belgium in 2023.

Traveling to Brussels by Car

Exploring at Your Own Pace

If you prefer the flexibility and freedom of traveling by car, Brussels is easily accessible by road, making it a convenient option for your visit. This section of the Brussels Travel Guide 2023 will provide you with essential information and tips for a seamless journey to the captivating capital of Belgium by car.

- **Road Networks:**

Brussels is well-connected to major European cities through an extensive road network.

Highways and motorways, such as the E19, E40, and E411, provide direct access to Brussels from neighboring countries.

- **Travel Documents and Insurance:**

Ensure you have a valid driver's license from your home country.

Check if an International Driving Permit is required, depending on your country of residence.

Verify that your car insurance covers travel abroad or consider purchasing temporary international coverage.

- **Route Planning:**

Plan your route in advance using a reliable navigation system or mapping app.

Consider using GPS navigation devices or smartphone apps for real-time traffic updates and alternative routes.

- **Traffic Regulations:**

Familiarize yourself with the traffic regulations of the countries you'll be passing through.

Observe speed limits, traffic signs, and regulations related to seat belts and child safety.

- **Parking in Brussels:**

Brussels has various parking options, including street parking, parking garages, and paid parking zones.

Familiarize yourself with the parking rules and fees in different areas of the city to avoid fines or unnecessary hassles.

- **Brussels Low Emission Zone (LEZ):**

Brussels has implemented a Low Emission Zone to improve air quality.

Check if your vehicle meets the emission standards required to enter the LEZ and, if necessary, register and obtain the required permits.

- **Traffic Congestion and Rush Hours:**

Brussels experiences traffic congestion, particularly during peak commuting hours.

Plan your travel accordingly and consider avoiding driving during rush hours to minimize delays.

Public Transportation and Park & Ride:

Brussels has an extensive public transportation network, including buses, trams, and the metro.

Consider utilizing Park & Ride facilities located on the outskirts of the city, where you can park your car and continue your journey by public transportation.

- **Day Trips and Exploring Beyond Brussels:**
Brussels serves as an excellent base for exploring other Belgian cities and attractions.
Plan day trips to nearby destinations such as Bruges, Ghent, Antwerp, or Waterloo, and enjoy the freedom of having your own vehicle.

- **Roadside Assistance:**
Familiarize yourself with the contact information for roadside assistance services in case of emergencies or breakdowns.
Keep essential supplies in your car, such as a spare tire, toolkit, first-aid kit, and emergency contact numbers.

Traveling to Brussels by car allows you to explore the city and its surrounding regions at your own pace, offering flexibility and convenience. Ensure you have the necessary travel documents, plan your route, and familiarize yourself with traffic regulations and parking options. Be mindful of traffic congestion and consider using public transportation or Park & Ride facilities when exploring Brussels city center. With your car, you can also embark on exciting day trips to nearby cities and attractions. Enjoy the freedom of the open road as you discover the rich culture, history, and culinary delights of Brussels and its neighboring regions in 2023.

Once you've arrived in Brussels, you'll want to navigate the city with ease and efficiency. This comprehensive guide to getting around Brussels in 2023 will provide you with essential information on the various transportation options available, helping you explore the captivating capital of Belgium with convenience and confidence.

Public Transportation

Brussels has a well extensive and efficient public means of transportation system, including buses, trams, and the metro.

Learn about the different types of tickets and passes available, such as single-use tickets, day passes, and multi-day cards, to suit your travel needs.

Familiarize yourself with the various public transportation lines, routes, and schedules to navigate the city effectively.

- **Metro:**

The Brussels metro system consists of four lines (1, 2, 5, and 6) that cover the city and its outskirts.

Discover the metro stations, transfers, and connections to reach popular attractions, neighborhoods, and landmarks.

- **Trams and Buses:**

Trams and buses are convenient modes of transportation for exploring Brussels, especially areas not covered by the metro.

Understand the tram and bus networks, routes, and schedules to reach specific destinations within the city.

- **Tickets and Fares:**

Learn about the different ticketing options, including contactless payment cards and smartphone apps, to simplify your travel experience. Explore the various fare zones and determine the appropriate ticket based on your journey's distance.

Taxis and Ride-Sharing Services

Taxis are readily available in Brussels and can be hailed on the street or found at designated taxi stands.

Ride-sharing services like Uber are also available for convenient point-to-point transportation.

Cycling

Brussels is a bicycle-friendly city with dedicated cycling paths and bike-sharing services.

Discover the options for renting bicycles and explore Brussels on two wheels, enjoying the city's sights at your own pace.

Walking

Brussels is a compact city, making it easily walkable, especially in the city center.

Take advantage of pleasant strolls through charming neighborhoods, discovering hidden gems along the way.

Car Rental and Driving

If you prefer driving in Brussels, there are car rental services available for convenience.

Be aware of traffic rules, parking regulations, and the Low Emission Zone (LEZ) restrictions in certain areas.

- **Accessibility:**

Brussels offers accessible transportation options for individuals with mobility challenges.

Discover the services and facilities available, such as wheelchair-accessible vehicles and barrier-free access to public transportation.

- **Planning Tips:**

Plan your routes using maps or navigation apps to optimize your time and minimize travel disruptions.

Consider peak commuting hours and potential traffic congestion when planning your travel within the city.

With this comprehensive guide to getting around Brussels, you'll have all the necessary information to navigate the city's transportation system with ease. Whether you choose public transportation, taxis, cycling, walking, or renting a car, Brussels offers a range of options to suit your preferences. Enjoy the convenience, accessibility, and efficiency of Brussels' transportation network as you explore the city's vibrant neighborhoods, iconic landmarks, and cultural treasures in 2023.

Chapter 3: Top Attractions in Brussels

• Atomium:

The iconic Atomium is a symbol of Brussels, representing scientific progress and modern architecture. Climb to the top for panoramic views of the city, explore the fascinating exhibitions, and learn about its significance as a legacy of the 1958 World Expo.

• Manneken Pis:

Don't miss the famous Manneken Pis, a small bronze statue that has become one of Brussels' most beloved icons. Discover the history behind this quirky landmark and witness its various costumes during festive occasions.

- **Royal Palace of Brussels:**

Marvel at the grandeur of the Royal Palace of Brussels, the official residence of the Belgian royal family. While you can't enter the palace itself, admire its stunning facade, explore the surrounding gardens, and witness the Changing of the Guard ceremony.

- **Saint-Michel and Gudule Cathedral:**

Visit the magnificent Saint-Michel and Gudule Cathedral, a stunning example of Gothic architecture. Explore its intricate interior, admire the stained glass windows, and soak in the spiritual atmosphere of this historic place of worship.

- **Belgian Comic Strip Center:**

Delve into the world of Belgian comics at the Belgian Comic Strip Center. Immerse yourself in the artistry and storytelling of famous comic characters like Tintin and the Smurfs through exhibits, original artwork, and interactive displays.

• Mini-Europe:

Embark on a miniature journey across Europe at Mini-Europe. This enchanting park features scaled-down replicas of famous European landmarks, allowing you to explore the continent in just a few hours.

• Royal Museums of Fine Arts of Belgium:

Art enthusiasts will be captivated by the Royal Museums of Fine Arts of Belgium. This complex houses a vast collection of masterpieces, including works by renowned artists like Bruegel, Rubens, and Magritte.

- ## Parc du Cinquantenaire:

Escape the urban bustle and unwind in the picturesque Parc du Cinquantenaire. This sprawling park offers beautiful gardens, wide avenues, and impressive monuments, making it an ideal spot for a stroll or a picnic.

- ## The Royal Greenhouses of Laeken:

During the limited opening period, marvel at the breathtaking beauty of the Royal Greenhouses of Laeken. Explore the stunning glass structures filled with rare and exotic plants, showcasing the royal family's passion for horticulture.

• Parks and Gardens in Brussels:

Brussels boasts numerous parks and gardens, providing tranquil oases amid the city's hustle and bustle. From the enchanting Botanical Garden to the expansive Bois de la Cambre, these green spaces offer opportunities for relaxation and outdoor activities.

Immerse yourself in the allure of Brussels as you visit these top attractions. With its mix of historical landmarks, artistic treasures, and natural beauty, the city promises an unforgettable experience. Whether you're drawn to architectural marvels, cultural icons, or serene green spaces, Brussels has something to captivate every visitor.

Chapter 4: Unveiling Brussels' Cultural Heritage

We will unveil the captivating cultural landscape of the city, guiding you through its museums, art galleries, architectural wonders, culinary delights, and exciting festivals.

Museums and Art Galleries

- **Magritte Museum**: Immerse yourself in the surreal world of René Magritte at the Magritte Museum. Housing the largest collection of the renowned Belgian surrealist artist, the museum showcases his thought-provoking paintings, sculptures, and personal belongings, offering a deeper understanding of his unique artistic vision.

- **Horta Museum:** Step into the exquisite world of Art Nouveau at the Horta Museum. This former home and studio of renowned architect Victor Horta beautifully showcases his innovative designs and architectural genius, providing insights into the Art Nouveau movement that flourished in Brussels during the end of the 19th and beginning of the 20th centuries.

- **Museum of Musical Instruments:** Discover the harmonious blend of music and culture at the Museum of Musical Instruments. This unique museum houses an extensive collection of instruments from various cultures and periods, allowing you to explore the rich history and diversity of musical traditions.

- **Royal Museums of Art and History:** Embark on a journey through time at the Royal Museums of Art and History. This vast museum complex encompasses diverse collections, including ancient artifacts, decorative arts, and archaeological discoveries, offering a comprehensive exploration of human history and cultural heritage.

Architecture and Landmarks

Brussels is a treasure trove of architectural wonders and landmarks that reflect its rich history and cultural heritage. Marvel at the following highlights:

- **Grand-Place:** Admire the awe-inspiring architecture and ornate facades of the Grand-Place, a UNESCO World Heritage site and the heart of Brussels' historic center.

- **Atomium:** Marvel at the futuristic design of the Atomium, a symbol of scientific progress and an iconic landmark of Brussels.

- **Saint-Michel and Gudule Cathedral:** Visit the magnificent Saint-Michel and Gudule Cathedral, a stunning Gothic masterpiece that has stood as a symbol of Brussels' religious heritage for centuries.

- **Cinquantenaire Arch:** Explore the impressive Cinquantenaire Arch and the surrounding park, which showcases monumental architecture and provides a picturesque backdrop for leisurely walks.

Belgian Cuisine and Beer Culture

Indulge in the culinary delights of Brussels and experience its renowned beer culture. Sample traditional Belgian dishes like moules-frites (mussels and fries), waffles, and indulgent chocolates. Explore the city's bustling food markets and cozy cafés, and savor the wide variety of Belgian beers, ranging from refreshing wheat beers to flavorful Trappist ales.

Festivals and Events in Brussels

Brussels comes alive with a vibrant calendar of festivals and events throughout the year. Don't miss: Brussels Jazz Festival: Immerse yourself in the melodious sounds of jazz during this annual festival held in January.

- **Belgian Beer Weekend**: Celebrate the rich beer heritage of Belgium during this three-day festival held in September, featuring an extensive selection of Belgian beers to taste and enjoy.

- **Christmas Markets:** Experience the enchanting atmosphere of Brussels' Christmas markets during the festive season, with charming stalls, sparkling lights, and seasonal treats.

Unveil Brussels' cultural heritage in 2023 and embark on a journey that celebrates art, architecture, cuisine, and festivities. Discover the city's museums, immerse yourself in its artistic treasures, marvel at architectural wonders, indulge in Belgian flavors, and join in the vibrant celebrations of its festivals and events. Brussels promises a captivating experience that will leave you with lasting memories and a deeper appreciation for its rich cultural tapestry.

Chapter 5: Shopping and Entertainment in Brussels

A World of Delights Brussels, the captivating capital of Belgium, offers a delightful array of shopping and entertainment options. From bustling shopping districts to local markets, indulgent chocolate and beer tastings, vibrant nightlife, and a thriving theater and performing arts scene, Brussels has something to satisfy every taste.

Rue Neuve and Shopping Districts

Step into the heart of Brussels' shopping scene on Rue Neuve, the city's main shopping street. Here, you'll find an extensive range of international brands, department stores, and fashionable boutiques. Explore the nearby shopping districts of Avenue Louise and Boulevard de Waterloo, known for their upscale fashion houses, luxury brands, and designer labels. Immerse yourself in a world of style, trends, and retail therapy as you browse through the diverse shops and boutiques.

Local Markets and Specialty Shops

To experience the local charm of Brussels, don't miss the vibrant markets and specialty shops scattered throughout the city. Visit Marché du Midi, a bustling market offering a vibrant mix of fresh produce, local delicacies, and unique items. Wander through the charming Sablon neighborhood and discover its antique shops, renowned for their exquisite craftsmanship and historical artifacts. Explore the treasures of artisanal boutiques, handicraft shops, and souvenir stores in lively markets like Place du Jeu de Balle and Marché des Antiquaires.

Belgian Chocolate and Beer Tastings

Indulge your senses with the decadent delights of Belgian chocolate and beer. Brussels is a paradise for chocolate lovers, with renowned chocolatiers offering an array of tempting treats. Embark on chocolate tastings and visits to chocolate factories, where you can sample a variety of flavors, textures, and pralines while gaining insights into the art of chocolate-making. Additionally, immerse yourself in Belgium's world-famous beer culture by visiting local breweries and beer bars. Participate in beer tastings to savor the rich flavors of traditional Belgian brews, from refreshing wheat beers to complex Trappist ales.

Nightlife and Entertainment

Brussels boasts a vibrant nightlife scene that caters to every taste. From trendy bars and clubs to cozy pubs and live music venues, the city offers endless opportunities for evening entertainment. Explore the vibrant neighborhoods of Saint-Géry, Flagey, and Place du Luxembourg, known for their lively nightlife and diverse range of venues. Enjoy a night out on the town, sipping cocktails, dancing to the latest beats, or simply soaking up the energetic atmosphere.

Theaters and Performing Arts

Immerse yourself in the world of theater and performing arts in Brussels. The city is home to numerous theaters, opera houses, and performance venues that showcase a wide range of productions, including plays, musicals, dance performances, and classical concerts. Experience the magic of performances at renowned venues like La Monnaie/De Munt, Théâtre Royal de Toone, and BOZAR, which hosts a diverse program of cultural events throughout the year.

In Brussels, shopping and entertainment go hand in hand, offering a world of delights to discover. Whether you're exploring the bustling shopping districts, indulging in chocolate and beer tastings, immersing yourself in the vibrant nightlife, or experiencing the magic of live performances, Brussels promises an unforgettable journey of enjoyment and discovery.

Chapter 6: Outdoor Activities and Recreation

Parks and Gardens in Brussels

Brussels, the captivating capital of Belgium, offers a variety of outdoor activities and opportunities for recreation. From picturesque parks to beautiful gardens, the city provides ample green spaces where visitors can relax, engage in sports, enjoy picnics, and immerse themselves in nature. In this Brussels Travel Guide 2023, we invite you to explore the parks and gardens that enhance the city's charm and provide a welcome respite from the bustling urban environment.

- **Bois de la Cambre:** Located on the outskirts of Brussels, Bois de la Cambre is a sprawling park that offers a peaceful retreat. Explore its vast green spaces, serene lakes, and picturesque pathways, ideal for leisurely walks, jogging, or cycling. Enjoy a boat ride on the lake, have a picnic on the grass, or simply relax amidst the beauty of nature.

- **Parc du Cinquantenaire:** Parc du Cinquantenaire is a grand urban park known for its monumental arch and beautifully landscaped gardens. Stroll through the park's avenues, admire the intricate flower beds, and marvel at the impressive arch. The park also houses several museums, making it a perfect combination of culture and outdoor recreation.

- **Brussels Park (Parc de Bruxelles):** Situated in the heart of Brussels, Brussels Park is a central green space that offers a tranquil escape from the bustling city streets. Take a leisurely walk along its paths, enjoy the shade of majestic trees, and discover charming statues and fountains. The park's proximity to the Royal Palace adds to its allure.

- **Josaphat Park:** Josaphat Park is a hidden gem nestled in the Schaerbeek district of Brussels. This expansive park features beautiful gardens, a large lake, playgrounds, and sports facilities. Take a jog along its trails, rent a paddleboat, or have a family picnic surrounded by nature's beauty.

- **Botanical Garden (Jardin Botanique):** Escape to the Botanical Garden, a peaceful oasis located near the city center. This enchanting garden showcases a wide variety of plant species from around the world, including impressive greenhouse structures. Take a stroll through the garden, enjoy the colorful blooms, and discover the diverse flora on display.

- **Woluwe Park:** Woluwe Park, situated in the eastern part of Brussels, is a vast green space that offers a range of recreational activities. With its rolling hills, serene ponds, and well-maintained trails, it is ideal for jogging, cycling, or simply enjoying a relaxing day outdoors. The park also features playgrounds, sports fields, and picnic areas.

- **King Baudouin Park (Parc Roi Baudouin):** Located near the Atomium, King Baudouin Park is a picturesque park that offers stunning views of the iconic landmark. Explore its expansive lawns, peaceful ponds, and beautiful sculptures. The park is also home to the Océade Waterpark and Mini-Europe, adding to its appeal as a family-friendly destination.

- **Japanese Tower and Chinese Pavilion:** Situated in the Laeken district, the Japanese Tower and Chinese Pavilion are part of the Royal Domain of Laeken. Surrounded by well-manicured gardens, these elegant structures provide a glimpse into Brussels' connection with Asian culture and make for a unique and picturesque visit

.

Brussels' parks and gardens offer a delightful escape from the urban environment, providing a serene and rejuvenating experience for visitors. Whether you seek a tranquil walk, a picnic with loved ones, or the opportunity to engage in sports and outdoor activities, these green spaces offer a sanctuary amidst the bustling city. Take a break, reconnect with nature, and enjoy the outdoor beauty that Brussels has to offer.

Cycling and Biking Routes in Brussels:

Explore the City on Two Wheels

Brussels, the vibrant capital of Belgium, is a city that welcomes cyclists with its well-developed cycling infrastructure and network of scenic routes. With dedicated cycling paths, bike-sharing programs, and a bicycle-friendly culture, exploring Brussels on two wheels offers a unique and enjoyable way to experience the city. In this Brussels Travel Guide 2023, we invite you to discover some of the best cycling and biking routes that will take you through the city's charming neighborhoods, iconic landmarks, and natural landscapes.

- **Brussels Green Belt:** Embark on a cycling adventure along the Brussels Green Belt (Brusselse Groene Wandeling), a 60-kilometer loop that encircles the city. This route takes you through parks, forests, and countryside areas, offering a peaceful and scenic ride. Explore the stunning Sonian

Forest (Forêt de Soignes), enjoy the picturesque Tervuren Park, and pass by charming villages on this idyllic green route.

- **Canal Bike Path:** Follow the Canal Bike Path that runs alongside the Brussels-Charleroi Canal (Canal de Bruxelles à Charleroi) and discover a different side of the city. This route takes you through industrial landscapes, and quaint neighborhoods, and offers glimpses of the city's rich industrial history. Enjoy the peaceful atmosphere as you pedal along the canal, passing by charming locks and historic bridges.

- **Royal Park:** Cycle through the heart of Brussels by exploring the Royal Park (Parc Royal). This central park offers a pleasant and car-free cycling experience, allowing you to enjoy the lush greenery and admire the stunning architecture of the Royal Palace. Pedal through the park's winding paths, take in the tranquil atmosphere and make a stop to visit the nearby museums and landmarks.

- **Woluwe Valley:** Discover the beauty of the Woluwe Valley (Vallée de la Woluwe), a picturesque green area that stretches along the Woluwe River. This cycling route takes you through serene parks, scenic paths, and charming neighborhoods. Enjoy the peaceful ambiance as you ride along the riverbanks, surrounded by nature and dotted with historical sites.
- **Bike-sharing:** Brussels offers bike-sharing programs that make it easy to explore the city on two wheels. Look for the villa! bicycles or other bike-sharing options available throughout the city. Rent a bike for a short period and explore at your own pace,

enjoying the convenience of easily accessible pick-up and drop-off points.

- **Urban Exploration:** Brussels' compact size makes it ideal for urban exploration on a bicycle. Discover the city's vibrant neighborhoods, including the historic center, the trendy Saint-Gilles, the bohemian Marolles, and the cosmopolitan European Quarter. Pedal along the city streets, stopping at charming cafés, bustling markets, and iconic landmarks along the way.

Safety Tips: When cycling in Brussels, prioritize your safety. Observe traffic rules, stay on designated bike paths whenever possible, and be mindful of pedestrians. Wear a helmet, use lights when cycling at night, and lock your bike securely when making stops. Familiarize yourself with the hand signals used by local cyclists to communicate their intentions.

Cycling in Brussels offers a unique perspective on the city's rich culture, history, and natural beauty. Enjoy the freedom of two wheels as you explore the city's diverse neighborhoods, iconic landmarks, and charming green spaces. Whether you're an experienced cyclist or a casual rider, Brussels invites you to embark on an exciting and eco-friendly adventure.

Boating and Water Activities

Boating and Water Activities in Brussels: Explore the City's Waterways Brussels, the vibrant capital of Belgium, offers a variety of boating and water activities that allow visitors to experience the city from a unique perspective. With its picturesque canals, tranquil lakes, and scenic waterways, Brussels provides opportunities for leisurely boat rides, kayaking adventures, and other exciting water-based activities. In this Brussels Travel Guide

2023, we invite you to discover the waterways of Brussels and the enjoyable experiences they offer.

- **Brussels Canal:** Explore the city's waterways by embarking on a boat tour along the Brussels Canal. Experience the charm of cruising through the heart of the city, passing by historic buildings, vibrant neighborhoods, and iconic landmarks. Learn about the city's history, architecture, and culture as you glide along the canal's tranquil waters.

- **Boat Tours:** Take advantage of the boat tour services available in Brussels, offering guided excursions that provide fascinating insights into the city's history and architecture. Join a narrated tour along the canals, learning about Brussels' heritage and passing by notable sites such as the Atomium, the Grand Place, and the Royal Palace.

- **Kayaking on the Waterways:** For a more active and immersive experience, go kayaking on Brussels' waterways. Rent a kayak and paddle along the canals, exploring the city at your own pace. Enjoy the tranquility of the water, observe the architectural beauty along the banks, and discover hidden corners and charming views that are only accessible by kayak.

- **Boating on Lakes and Ponds:** Brussels is home to several lakes and ponds where you can enjoy boating and other water activities. Visit Bois de la Cambre, a beautiful park with a lake where you can rent rowboats and pedal boats. Explore the serene waters, surrounded by lush greenery and stunning views. **Additionally,** Woluwe Park and Parc du Cinquantenaire offer boating opportunities, providing a serene escape within the city.

- **Water Sports:** Brussels also offers opportunities for water sports enthusiasts. If you're seeking a more active adventure, try stand-up paddleboarding (SUP) on the city's lakes or participate in wakeboarding activities at cable parks located on the outskirts of Brussels. These thrilling water sports experiences add a touch of adrenaline to your visit.

- **Fishing:** For those who enjoy fishing, Brussels offers various spots where you can cast a line and try your luck. Visit lakes and ponds such as Woluwe Park and Bois de la Cambre, which are known for their fishing opportunities. Familiarize yourself with local fishing regulations and obtain the necessary permits before embarking on a fishing excursion.

Safety and Regulations: When participating in water activities in Brussels, it is essential to prioritize safety. Follow any rules and regulations set by boat tour operators, rental services, or water sports providers. Ensure to put appropriate safety equipment, such as life jackets, when required. If you're kayaking or participating in water sports independently, be mindful of other water users, respect designated areas, and be aware of weather conditions and water currents.

Exploring Brussels' waterways provides a unique perspective on the city's beauty and allows for a peaceful and enjoyable experience. Whether you're taking a relaxing boat tour, kayaking along the canals, or engaging in water sports, Brussels offers a range of water-based activities to suit every interest. So, dive in, make a splash, and create memorable moments as you discover the aquatic side of Brussels in 2023.

Sports and Recreation Facilities

Sports and Recreation Facilities in Brussels: Stay Active and Have Fun in Brussels, the dynamic capital of Belgium, offers a wide range of sports and recreation facilities to keep visitors active and entertained. Whether you're a sports enthusiast, fitness enthusiast, or simply looking for some recreational fun, Brussels has something for everyone. In this Brussels Travel Guide 2023, we invite you to explore the city's sports and recreation facilities that will ensure an enjoyable and active stay.

- **Sports Centers and Gyms**: Brussels is home to numerous sports centers and gyms, offering state-of-the-art facilities and a variety of fitness activities. Join a fitness class, hit the weights, or take advantage of the cardio machines and swimming pools available. Many centers also offer amenities like saunas and steam rooms, providing a well-rounded fitness experience.

- **Outdoor Sports Facilities:** Enjoy outdoor sports at Brussels' many recreational parks and facilities. Take advantage of the city's well-maintained sports fields, tennis courts, basketball courts, and running tracks. Whether you prefer a friendly game with friends or a more competitive match, these facilities cater to all levels of skill and provide a chance to engage in your favorite sports.

- **Cycling and Biking Paths:** Brussels boasts an extensive network of cycling and biking paths that span the city. Rent a bicycle and explore the city's scenic routes, enjoying a leisurely ride along tree-lined avenues, canals, and parks. For the more adventurous, venture outside the city to experience challenging mountain biking trails and scenic countryside routes.
- **Swimming Pools:** Cool off and enjoy a refreshing swim in one of Brussels' swimming pools. The city offers a variety of indoor and outdoor pools, ranging from

Olympic-sized facilities to leisure pools for the whole family. Whether you're looking to do laps, relax by the poolside, or have some fun with water slides and splash zones, there's a swimming pool to suit your needs.

- **Golf Courses:** Tee off at one of Brussels' golf courses, which provides an excellent opportunity for golf enthusiasts to practice their swing amidst beautiful surroundings. Enjoy a round of golf at courses designed for all skill levels, accompanied by scenic views and well-maintained fairways. Some courses also offer professional instruction for beginners or those looking to improve their game.

- **Adventure Parks:** For an adrenaline-filled experience, visit adventure parks located within and around Brussels. Test your limits with zip lines, climbing walls, rope courses, and other thrilling activities. These parks provide an exciting day out for families, groups of friends, or even team-building activities.

- **Water Sports:** Take advantage of Brussels' water sports facilities for a unique and refreshing experience. Try your hand at sailing, windsurfing, or paddleboarding on the city's lakes and waterways. Some facilities offer lessons and equipment rental, making it accessible for beginners and experienced water sports enthusiasts alike.

- **Recreational Parks:** Brussels boasts several recreational parks that offer a wide range of activities for all ages. From picnics and leisurely walks to playgrounds and fitness stations, these parks provide a perfect setting for relaxation and recreation. Popular parks include Bois de la Cambre, Woluwe Park, and Parc du Cinquantenaire.

When visiting sports and recreation facilities, be sure to check their operating hours, availability of equipment rentals, and any admission requirements or fees. Remember to stay hydrated, wear appropriate sports attire, and follow safety guidelines for each activity.

Brussels provides ample opportunities to stay active, have fun, and pursue your favorite sports and recreational activities. Whether you're a sports enthusiast or simply looking to enjoy some leisurely fun, the city offers a diverse range of options to cater to all interests and fitness levels. So, get ready to engage in exciting sports, stay fit, and make the most of your visit to Brussels.

Chapter 7: Practical Information

Accommodation Options in Brussels

When planning your visit to Brussels, it's essential to choose the right accommodation that suits your needs and preferences. Brussels offers a wide range of accommodation options, from luxurious hotels to budget-friendly hostels and cozy guesthouses. In this Brussels Travel Guide 2023, we provide practical information on accommodation options to help you make an informed decision.

Hotels

Brussels boasts a diverse selection of hotels, ranging from international chains to boutique establishments. The city center offers a concentration of hotels, making it a convenient base for exploring the city's attractions. Prices vary depending on the hotel's location, amenities, and star rating. On average, expect to pay around €80-€200 per night for a mid-range hotel room in central Brussels. Luxury hotels can cost upwards of €200 per night, while budget-friendly options start at around €50 per night.

Recommended hotels:

- **The Hotel Brussels:** Located near Avenue Louise, this luxury hotel offers panoramic views of the city skyline and excellent amenities.

- **NH Collection Brussels Centre:** Situated in the heart of the historic center, this modern hotel provides easy access to major attractions and comfortable rooms.
- **Meininger Hotel Brussels City Center:** A budget-friendly option located near the Brussels-North train station, offering affordable private and shared rooms.

Hostels

If you're seeking budget-friendly accommodation or prefer a social atmosphere, hostels are a popular choice. Brussels has a range of hostels scattered throughout the city, with prices varying based on location and facilities. Expect to pay around €20-€40 per night for a bed in a shared dormitory room. Private rooms in hostels are also available at higher rates.

Recommended hostels:

- **Generation Europe Youth Hostel:** Located near the European Quarter, this hostel offers an affordable dormitory and private rooms, along with common areas for socializing.
- **Brussels Hello Hostel:** Situated in the city center, this lively hostel provides a welcoming atmosphere, comfortable beds, and communal spaces for guests to mingle.

Guesthouses and Bed and Breakfasts

For a more intimate and homey experience, consider staying in a guesthouse or bed and breakfast. These accommodations offer personalized service and a cozy ambiance. Prices vary depending on location, amenities, and the level of service provided. Expect to pay around €60-€150 per night for a room in a guesthouse or bed and breakfast.

Recommended guesthouses

- **B&B Le Coup de Coeur:** Located in the trendy Saint-Gilles neighborhood, this charming guesthouse offers comfortable rooms and a delicious breakfast.
- **B&B Living in Brûsel, Urban B&B:** Situated near the European Quarter, this modern bed and breakfast provides stylish rooms and a warm, welcoming atmosphere.

Apartment Rentals

If you prefer a more independent and self-catering experience, renting an apartment can be an excellent option. Brussels has a wide range of apartments available for short-term rentals, allowing you to have your own space and amenities. The Prices vary depending on location, size, and level of luxury. On average, expect to pay around €70-€150 per night for a centrally located apartment.

Recommended apartment rental platforms

- **Airbnb:** Offers a variety of apartments and private rooms across the city.
- **Booking.com:** Provides a range of apartment options with different amenities and price points.

When booking accommodation, consider factors such as proximity to public transportation, attractions, and amenities that are important to you. It's advisable to book before the day, especially during peak travel seasons, to secure the accommodation of your choice.

Please note that the prices mentioned are estimated averages and may vary based on factors such as seasonality, availability, and specific hotel or property policies.

In Brussels, you'll find a variety of accommodation options to suit every budget and preference. Whether you're seeking luxury, affordability, or a cozy home-like atmosphere, the city offers a range of choices to ensure a comfortable and enjoyable stay.

Restaurants and Dining

Restaurants and Dining in Brussels is a Gastronomic Adventure in Brussels, the culinary capital of Belgium, is a haven for food enthusiasts, offering a diverse and vibrant dining scene. From renowned Michelin-starred restaurants to charming cafés and traditional Belgian eateries, the city caters to every taste and budget.

- **Belgian Cuisine**: Indulge in the flavors of authentic Belgian cuisine, known for its rich and hearty dishes. Don't miss the opportunity to savor traditional favorites such as moules-frites (mussels with fries), carbonnade flamande (beef stew), and waterzooi (creamy chicken or fish stew). Pair your meal with a selection of local beers or indulge in a decadent serving of Belgian chocolate for dessert.

- **Fine Dining:** Brussels boasts an array of world-class restaurants where talented chefs push the boundaries of gastronomy. Experience innovative cuisine and exceptional dining experiences at Michelin-starred establishments such as Bon-Bon, Comme Chez Soi, and The Jane. These restaurants showcase the finest ingredients, intricate techniques, and artistic presentations that will tantalize your taste buds.

- **Brussels' Neighborhood Eateries:** Explore the city's vibrant neighborhoods and discover hidden culinary gems. From the trendy

Saint-Gilles and Ixelles districts to the historical Marolles and Sablon neighborhoods, you'll find an abundance of local eateries offering diverse cuisines. Sample international flavors, trendy fusion dishes, or opt for traditional Belgian bistros that serve classic dishes with a contemporary twist.

- **Seafood and Fish:** With its proximity to the North Sea, Brussels is renowned for its seafood and fish dishes. Indulge in a platter of fresh oysters, enjoy succulent shrimp croquettes, or feast on a seafood platter featuring an array of delicacies like crab, lobster, and langoustines. Visit seafood-focused restaurants and fish markets to experience the best of Brussels' maritime offerings.

- **Street Food and Markets:** Immerse yourself in the lively street food culture of Brussels.

Explore local markets like Marché du Midi or Place du Jeu de Balle, where you can sample a variety of street snacks, including Belgian waffles, frites (fries), and crispy Belgian-style waffles dusted with powdered sugar. Don't forget to try the famous Belgian fries, served with an assortment of flavorful sauces.

- **International Cuisine:** Brussels is a melting pot of cultures, reflected in its diverse culinary scene. Experience flavors from around the world, with an abundance of international restaurants offering cuisines from Italian and French to Japanese, Moroccan, and beyond. Whether you're craving sushi, pasta, tapas, or exotic spices, you'll find an array of options to satisfy your cravings.

- **Cafés and Brasseries:** Take a break from exploring and relax at one of Brussels' charming cafés and brasseries. Enjoy a leisurely breakfast with freshly baked pastries, sip on a cup of aromatic coffee, or indulge in a light lunch. Immerse yourself in the café culture, where you can savor the atmosphere, people-watch, and experience the city's vibrant energy.

- **Beer Culture:** No visit to Brussels is complete without exploring its legendary beer culture. Discover traditional Belgian beer bars, known as "cafés," where you can sample a vast selection of local brews, from Trappist ales and fruity lambics to strong abbey beers. Visit beer-focused establishments, such as Delirium Café, known for its extensive beer menu featuring over 2,000 varieties.

When dining in Brussels, keep in mind that reservations are recommended, especially for popular restaurants and during peak dining hours.

Tipping is customary, typically around 10% of the total bill, although some establishments may include a service charge.

Brussels' culinary scene offers a tantalizing array of flavors, from traditional Belgian fare to international delicacies, ensuring a gastronomic adventure for every palate. Embrace the city's passion for food, explore its diverse dining options, and savor the unforgettable culinary experiences that await you.

Health and Safety Tips

Ensuring a Safe and Enjoyable Visit to Brussels When traveling to Brussels, it's essential to prioritize your health and safety to ensure a worry-free and enjoyable visit. As with any destination, being aware of potential risks and taking necessary precautions is important. In this Brussels Travel Guide 2023, we provide comprehensive health and safety tips to help you have a safe and memorable experience in the city.

1. **Travel Insurance:** Before your trip, consider obtaining comprehensive travel insurance that covers medical expenses, trip cancellation, and lost or stolen belongings. It provides peace of mind in case of unexpected incidents or emergencies.

2. **Health Precautions:**Check with your healthcare provider for any required vaccinations or recommended immunizations for traveling to Belgium.

- Pack a basic first aid kit with essential items such as band-aids, pain relievers, anti-diarrheal medication, and any necessary prescription medications.

- Familiarize yourself with the location of nearby hospitals, clinics, and pharmacies in case of medical emergencies.

3. COVID-19 Precautions:

Stay informed about the latest travel advisories and guidelines related to COVID-19, including vaccination requirements, testing protocols, and quarantine regulations.

- Follow local health authority guidelines regarding mask-wearing, social distancing, and hygiene practices.
- Carry hand sanitizer and use it regularly, especially before eating or touching your face.
- Stay updated on any changes to travel restrictions or entry requirements.

4. General Safety Tips:

Be aware of your surroundings and keep an eye on your belongings at all times, especially in crowded areas and on public transportation.

- Use reputable transportation services and official taxi stands. Avoid unlicensed or unofficial taxis.
- Keep a photocopy of your passport, identification, and other important documents, and store them separately from the originals.
- Stay in well-lit areas and avoid walking alone late at night, particularly in unfamiliar neighborhoods.
- Be cautious of scams or pickpocketing attempts. Keep your valuables secure and be mindful of your personal belongings.

5. Emergency Contacts:

Save emergency contact numbers, including local police, medical services, and your embassy or consulate, in your phone or write them down in case of emergencies.

- Familiarize yourself with the local emergency number, which is 112 in Belgium.

6. Weather Precautions:

Check the weather forecast and plan accordingly, especially during extreme weather conditions.

- Carry appropriate clothing and accessories to protect against rain, cold, or excessive heat.

7. Transportation Safety:

Use licensed and reputable transportation options. Follow traffic rules and use designated pedestrian crossings when walking.

- When using public transportation, be mindful of your belongings and be aware of any pickpocketing risks.

8. Respect Local Customs and Laws:

Familiarize yourself with local customs, traditions, and laws to ensure you respect the local culture and avoid any unintentional offenses.

It's important by staying informed, taking necessary precautions, and exercising common sense, you can have a safe and enjoyable visit to Brussels. Embrace the city's charm, immerse yourself in its vibrant culture, and create lasting memories while prioritizing your health and safety.

Communication and Internet Access in Brussels

Staying Connected when visiting Brussels, staying connected and having access to communication services is essential for a smooth and enjoyable trip. Whether you need to make calls, access the internet, or navigate your way through the city, here's a comprehensive guide to communication and internet access in Brussels for the Brussels Travel Guide 2023:

1. Mobile Networks and SIM Cards:

Brussels has excellent mobile network coverage from major providers such as Proximus, Orange, and Base. Check if your mobile phone is unlocked to use local SIM cards.

Purchase a prepaid SIM card from one of the providers upon arrival to have local calling and data services. You'll need to present identification to register the SIM card.

2. Internet Access:

Most hotels, cafes, and restaurants in Brussels offer free Wi-Fi access for their customers. Look for signage indicating Wi-Fi availability or inquire with the staff.

- Brussels also has several public Wi-Fi hotspots, including in parks and public spaces. Some may require registration or provide limited free access.

3. Internet Cafes:

Internet cafes are available in Brussels if you need a dedicated space for Internet access. These establishments offer computers with internet connections for a fee.

4. Roaming:

If you prefer to use your own mobile service provider, check their roaming packages to ensure cost-effective usage while in Brussels. Be aware of data roaming charges to avoid unexpected costs.

5. Phone Calls:

To make international calls from Brussels, dial the exit code of your home country followed by the country code and the local number. The exit code for most countries is "+" or "00."

If you need to make local calls within Belgium, simply dial the local number.

6. Messaging and VoIP:

Messaging apps like WhatsApp, Facebook Messenger, and Viber can be used over Wi-Fi or mobile data to stay in touch with friends and family. Voice over Internet Protocol (VoIP) services such as Skype and FaceTime can be used to make voice and video calls over the Internet, which can be a cost-effective option for international calls.

7. Postal Services:

If you need to send mail or postcards, visit one of the local post offices (La Poste) in Brussels. Post offices are typically open on weekdays and Saturday mornings.

8. Language Considerations:

The official speaking languages of Brussels are French and Dutch. The English language is widely spoken, especially in tourist areas, hotels, and restaurants.

Remember to check with your mobile service provider regarding international coverage and roaming charges before your trip. Additionally, be mindful of your data usage to avoid excessive charges.

By utilizing these communication options and staying connected, you can navigate Brussels with ease, keep in touch with loved ones, and make the most of your visit.

Money-Saving Tips and Budgeting

Getting the Most Out of Your Experience Traveling to Brussels doesn't have to break the bank. With careful planning effectively and smart choices, you can make your trip affordable and enjoyable.

1. **Plan and Research:**
   - Start by creating a budget for your trip, including transportation, accommodation, meals, activities, and souvenirs.

- Research the cost of attractions, public transportation, and dining options in Brussels to have a realistic idea of expenses.

2. **Travel During Off-Peak Seasons**:

- Consider traveling to Brussels during off-peak seasons, such as spring or autumn, to take advantage of lower accommodation and flight prices.
- Prices for attractions and activities may also be more affordable during non-peak times.

3. **Accommodation:**

- Look for budget-friendly accommodations, such as hostels, guesthouses, or apartments, which can offer significant savings compared to luxury hotels.
- Consider staying outside the city center and using public transportation to access attractions if it means finding more affordable accommodations.

4. Dining:

- Explore local markets and grocery stores to buy snacks, fresh produce, and picnic supplies. Enjoying a meal in one of Brussels' beautiful parks can be a cost-effective and enjoyable option.

- Take good advantage of lunch specials or prix-fixe menus at restaurants, which often offer the same quality of food at a lower price compared to dinner options.

- Try street food, such as Belgian waffles or frites, which can be a delicious and affordable way to taste local flavors.

5. Public Transportation:

- Utilize Brussels' efficient public transportation system, including buses, trams, and metros, which offer affordable options for getting around the city.

- Consider purchasing a Brussels Card, which provides unlimited access to public transportation and discounts on attractions, allowing you to save money while sightseeing.

1. Free and Low-Cost Activities:

- Take advantage of the numerous free attractions and activities in Brussels, such as visiting parks, exploring public art installations, or admiring the city's stunning architecture.

- Check if any museums or attractions offer discounted or free entry on specific days or times.

6. City Passes and Discount Cards:

- Look into city passes or discount cards, such as the Brussels Card, which provide discounted entry to attractions and public transportation. These can be cost-effective if you plan to visit multiple sites.

1. Souvenirs and Shopping:

- Avoid touristy areas for souvenir shopping, as prices tend to be inflated. Instead, explore local markets and specialty shops for unique and reasonably priced souvenirs.

- Consider purchasing edible souvenirs like Belgian chocolates or beers, which can be a delicious and budget-friendly option.

7. Tipping:

- Check the bill to see if a service charge is included before tipping in restaurants. If service is exceptional, leaving a small tip is appreciated but not mandatory.

8. Stay Hydrated and Carry a Reusable Water Bottle:

- Save money by carrying a reusable water bottle and refilling it at public drinking fountains or asking for tap water at restaurants instead of purchasing bottled water.

Remember, budgeting doesn't mean sacrificing experiences. By implementing these money-saving tips and prioritizing your expenses, you can make the most of your visit to Brussels while staying within your budget. With careful effective planning, you'll have a fantastic and affordable trip in 2023.

Chapter 8: Beyond Brussels

Beyond Brussels: Day Trips from the City

While Brussels offers a wealth of attractions and experiences, there are also several captivating destinations located within a short distance from the city. In this Brussels Travel Guide 2023, we present a comprehensive list of day trip options that will allow you to explore the beauty and history of Belgium beyond Brussels:

1. **Ghent:** Located just a short train ride from Brussels, Ghent is a picturesque city known for its medieval architecture, charming canals, and vibrant cultural scene. Visit the famous Saint Bavo's Cathedral, stroll along the scenic Graslei and Korenlei waterfront, and explore the historic Gravensteen Castle. Ghent is also home to numerous museums, art galleries, and delightful restaurants, offering a perfect blend of history and contemporary charm.

2. **Bruges:** Considered one of Europe's most well-preserved medieval cities, Bruges is a UNESCO World Heritage site that captivates visitors with its cobbled streets, picturesque canals, and stunning architecture. Take a leisurely boat tour, visit the iconic Belfry Tower, and explore the historic Markt Square.

Don't forget to indulge in delicious Belgian chocolates and try the famous Bruges waffles. Bruges is easily accessible from Brussels by train.

3. **Antwerp:** Known for its vibrant fashion scene, Antwerp is a lively city with a rich cultural heritage. Discover the magnificent Cathedral of Our Lady, explore the trendy fashion district, and visit the Royal Museum of Fine Arts. Don't miss the chance to stroll along the Scheldt River and visit the famous Antwerp Central Station, considered one of the world's most beautiful train stations. Antwerp can be reached from Brussels within an hour by train.

4. **Waterloo:** History enthusiasts will appreciate a day trip to Waterloo, where the famous Battle of Waterloo took place in 1815. Explore the visitor center and museum dedicated to the battle, visit the iconic Lion's

Mound, and gain insight into this significant event that changed the course of European history. Waterloo is easily accessible by train from Brussels.

5. **Leuven:** A vibrant university city, Leuven is known for its stunning architecture, lively atmosphere, and historic sites. Marvel at the UNESCO-listed Town Hall, explore the beautiful gardens of the Arenberg Castle and visit the renowned Stella Artois Brewery. Leuven's charming streets are lined with cafes, restaurants, and boutiques, creating a delightful ambiance for visitors. It is a short distance train ride away from the beautiful Brussels.

6. **Namur:** Located at the confluence of the Meuse and Sambre rivers, Namur is the capital of the Wallonia region and offers a blend of history, nature, and culture. Explore the medieval Namur Citadel, visit the

imposing St-Aubin's Cathedral, and stroll along the charming streets of the historic city center. Enjoy panoramic views from the Citadel's viewpoint and take a leisurely boat ride on the rivers. Namur can be reached from Brussels by train.

Other Nearby Destinations: If you have more time to explore, consider additional day trips to destinations such as Mechelen, Dinant, Leuven, or the Ardennes region, known for its stunning natural landscapes and outdoor activities.

When planning your day trips, check the train schedules and consider purchasing a day pass or individual tickets in advance to ensure a smooth and convenient journey.

These day trips from Brussels offer a glimpse into the diverse and captivating beauty of Belgium. Each destination has its own unique charm, history, and attractions, allowing you to expand your exploration and make the most of your visit to Belgium in 2023.

Conclusion and Final Tips

Unveiling the Treasures of Brussels as your journey through Brussels comes to a close, this Brussels Travel Guide 2023 would like to leave you with some final tips and recommendations to make your experience truly memorable:

Hidden Gems and Local Recommendations

- Brussels is a city filled with hidden gems waiting to be discovered. Venture off the beaten path and explore lesser-known neighborhoods like Saint-Géry or Saint-Boniface, where you'll find unique shops, local markets, and charming cafés.

- Seek out local recommendations for authentic experiences, whether it's trying a beloved neighborhood bakery, attending a local music festival, or exploring a hidden courtyard.

Interacting with locals can unveil the true spirit of Brussels.

Traveling Responsibly

- Respect the local culture and be mindful of your impact on the environment. Dispose of waste properly and follow sustainable travel practices.
- Support local businesses, artisans, and restaurants to contribute to the local economy and foster authentic connections with the community.

Useful Phrases in French and Dutch

- Learning a few basic phrases in French and Dutch can go a long way in Brussels. Use greetings like "Bonjour" (French) or

"Goedemorgen" (Dutch) and phrases such as "Merci" (Thank you) or "Alstublieft" (Please/Here you go) to connect with locals and show respect for their language and culture.

Metro Map of Brussels

- Familiarize yourself with the Brussels metro map, which provides a convenient and efficient way to navigate the city. The metro system is well-connected, making it easy to reach various attractions and neighborhoods.

Currency and Money Matters

- The currency in Brussels is the Euro (€). Be aware of current exchange rates and inform your bank or credit card company of your travel plans to avoid any issues with international transactions.

- ATMs are widely available throughout the city, and credit cards are generally accepted at most establishments. However, it's advisable to carry some cash for smaller businesses or in case of emergencies.

As you bid farewell to Brussels, cherish the memories created during your visit. The city's rich history, vibrant culture, and warm hospitality leave a lasting impression on every traveler.

Remember, this Brussels Travel Guide 2023 is just a starting point. Embrace your sense of adventure, be open to unexpected discoveries, and allow yourself to get lost in the charm of Brussels. The city's hidden gems and local recommendations are waiting to be explored, offering you a truly authentic experience.

Bon voyage and enjoy your remarkable journey through Brussels!

Printed in Great Britain
by Amazon

37351061R00076